CUTTING-EDGE STEM

TOP STEM CAREERS IN SCIENCE

ANASTASIA SUEN

ROSEN
PUBLISHING®

New York

Published in 2015 by The Rosen Publishing Group, Inc.
29 East 21st Street, New York, NY 10010

First Edition

Library of Congress Cataloging-in-Publication Data

Suen, Anastasia, author.
Top STEM careers in science/Anastasia Suen.
    pages cm. — (Cutting-edge STEM careers)
Audience: 7-12.
Includes bibliographical references and index.
ISBN 978-1-4777-7664-3 (library bound) —
ISBN 978-1-4777-7666-7 (pbk.) —
ISBN 978-1-4777-7667-4 (6-pack)
1. Science—Vocational guidance—Juvenile literature.
2. Technology—Vocational guidance—Juvenile litera-
ture. 3. Engineering—Vocational guidance—Juvenile
literature. 4. Mathematics—Vocational guidance—
Juvenile literature. I. Title.
Q147.S79 2015
502.3—dc23

2013051188

Manufactured in Malaysia

CONTENTS

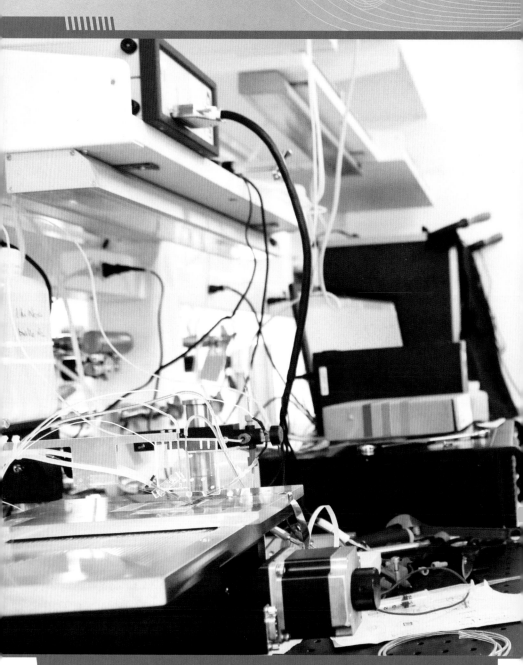

Staff scientist Cheng Xiang (*foreground*) and research engineer Dan Guevarra perform a CO_2 reduction experiment developing solar fuels at the California Institute of Technology.

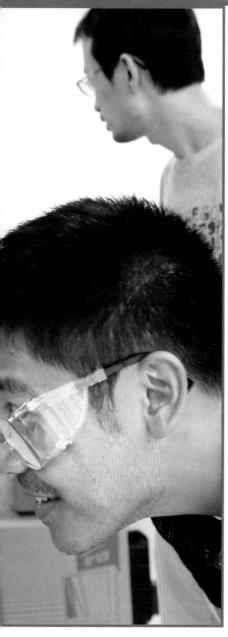

At a recent Intel International Science and Engineering Fair (ISEF) seventeen-year-old Henry Wanjune Lin, a student of Caddo Parish Magnet High School in Shreveport, Louisiana, won $50,000 for his project. He called it "Cool Core Bias in Sunyaev-Zel'dovich Galaxy Cluster Surveys."

So what did he do to win? Henry simulated thousands of clusters of galaxies. He compared his own mathematical predictions about galaxy clusters with what astronomers have observed using telescopes. By doing so he discovered that the scientists are more likely to find galaxies that have cooler-than-usual core temperatures. The award description read, "These finalists were selected for their commitment to innovation in tackling challenging scientific questions, using authentic research practices, and creating solutions to the problems of tomorrow."

Henry competed with students from all over the world. The 1,600 ISEF finalists were selected from the winners of science fairs in more than 70 countries, regions, and territories. Henry tied for second in the entire competition.

Henry also won best in category for his science fair project. He was given $5,000, and his school was awarded a $1,000 grant. In addition, Henry won $3,000 for first place in the physics and astronomy category. Have you added it up yet? One science fair project earned seventeen-year-old Henry $58,000!

This wasn't the first time Henry had been an ISEF finalist. The previous year he entered a different astronomy project. That one was called, "A Generalized Holographic Model of Cosmic Accelerated Expansion." There were 1,500 finalists at ISEF that year. All of them had worked their way up from the science fairs in their home towns.

Henry also placed second in the physics and astronomy category and was awarded $1,500. In addition, he was given a second-place award by the American Statistical Association (ASA). This ASA prize for best use of statistics in a project came with a certificate and $500. Henry received another $500 second-place prize for scientific merit from the Bok Awards for Astronomy. He also won $1,200 from the American Association of Physics Teachers and the American Physical Society. The National Aeronautics and Space Administration (NASA) gave him $1,000 for his project. That year, Henry was also a CERN Special Award Winner. His prize was an all-expenses paid trip to the European Organization for Nuclear Research (CERN) in Switzerland.

The science and math classes that you take in school can lead to rewarding science, technology, engineering, and mathematics (STEM) careers. STEM is in high demand by employers today, as you'll see when you explore the top science careers in this resource.

Do you want to protect the planet? You can work as an environmental scientist and specialist, an environmental science and protection technician, a hydrologist, a water quality technician, or an environmental health and safety technician. In a career as an agricultural and food scientist or technician, you can feed the world.

Microbiologists and medical scientists save lives. As a biochemist, a biophysicist, a biological technician, a chemist, or a materials scientist you can create something that will change the world. The possibilities, as you'll read in the following sections, are endless.

CHAPTER ONE

Preparing for a STEM Career in Science

The winner at a recent Intel ISEF competition was fifteen-year-old high school freshman Jack Andraka. He received a $75,000 scholarship for inventing a new way to detect pancreatic cancer. He also won the Gordon E. Moore Award, given to the "Best of the Best." So how did he do it? It all started in sixth grade when Jack had to do a science fair project for school. "I was immediately hooked!" Jack wrote on the *Society for Science* blog. After completing his project, he accompanied his older brother to the ISEF competition later that year. "The quality of the projects, the fact that science and math kids were so cool and interesting, the excitement of the event, and watching the awards ceremony left a deep impression on me," he said. "I dreamed of becoming an Intel ISEF finalist!"

To make that dream a reality, Jack went to as many science fairs as he could. Also, he said, he attended "the Intel Science Talent Search's Public Exhibition of Projects every year to listen to the finalists and learn how to make my presentations more interesting."

The science fair project that won that year's award was inspired by a tragedy. After a close family friend died from pancreatic cancer, Jack did some research on the disease. He discovered that in 85 percent of diagnosed cases, the person has only a 2 percent chance of survival. "My idea was to find a method of detecting the cancer early and thus reduce mortality rates," he said.

Jack took something that his father was working on (carbon nanotubes) and combined it with what his biology teacher said about antibodies and came up with a new idea. He wrote up an experimental protocol and e-mailed it to two hundred researchers. Only one replied: Anirban Maitra, a Johns Hopkins pathologist and pancreatic cancer researcher, who invited the teen to come work in his lab.

Jack went to the lab every day after school and on Saturdays for months. He mixed single-walled carbon nanotubes with antibodies of the cancer biomarker mesothelin. And after seven months, it worked. The result was "a sensor that can detect mesothelin and thus pancreatic, ovarian, and lung cancer for 3 cents in 5 minutes," said Jack. "It is 168 times faster, more than 26,000 times less expensive, and more than 400 times more sensitive than the current method of detection!"

Jack Andraka speaks after receiving *Smithsonian* magazine's first annual American Ingenuity Award for youth achievement on November 28, 2012, in Washington, D.C.

After winning the top prize at ISEF, Jack was also honored by *Smithsonian* magazine, which gave him the youth achievement Smithsonian American Ingenuity Award. *Smithsonian* reported that during his sophomore year of high school, Jack was "in high demand, giving TED talks and speaking at international ideas festivals."

What ideas did Jack share? On the *Society for Science* blog, he recommended that students "pick a topic they love because they will be spending a lot of

THE INTEL INTERNATIONAL SCIENCE AND ENGINEERING FAIR

The Intel International Science and Engineering Fair (ISEF) is the world's largest international high school science competition. In 1950, when it started, it was known as the National Science Fair. Then, as now, it was run by the Society for Science and the Public.

Every student who participates has won a science fair in his or her own community. Now that the competition is international, there are more than seventy countries, regions, and territories that send their science fair winners.

time with it." As for working in a professional lab, Jack had this advice: "If you are looking for a lab, be prepared with a timeline, budget, material list, and experimental design."

Your Science Fair Project Can Lead to a Career

As you will see on the following pages of this resource, recent ISEF winners have had some amazing ideas. These are your peers, so let them inspire you. In an ISEF press release, Elizabeth Marincola, president of the Society for Science and the Public wrote, "As this competition gets bigger, students not previously involved in such competitions can realize that independent research is both possible and rewarding."

What you do now does matter. Your science fair project can lead to a lucrative career. Your future begins now. There are many possible career paths. You can be trained to work as a technician after earning your high school degree. You can find entry-level work in science with a two-year associate's degree or a bachelor's degree. You can continue your education

There are so many rewarding STEM science career paths for you to choose after graduation. Who knows what great discoveries you can make?

and go to graduate school to earn a master's degree or a doctorate. There is a demand for STEM careers at every level of education.

While you are in high school, take both science and math classes. Science will be the core of your work, but you will need the math for analysis. Much of the work in the lab is done on computers, so you will need advanced training there as well.

Many of the other core classes you need to take to graduate will also serve you well in your career. The writing skills you learn in English class will help you with the many reports you will have to write on the job. You will need the skills you learn in speech class to give presentations about your work. (They can also help you get the job in the first place.) Your economics class will help you understand that business is controlled by supply and demand.

STEM Opportunities

The demand for STEM careers is there, so keep your eye out for any opportunities you can find in your community. Join the science club in high school and enter the school science fair each year. Immerse yourself in STEM over the summer. There are STEM programs for all ages offered each summer around the country. Do a Web search for "Summer STEM Programs/Camps" and find a program near you.

Petaluma High School senior Kelly Jackson solders a wireless transceiver for her water quality measurement system in the Sonoma State University Science and Technology High School Internship Program.

Let your interest in STEM help pay for your college degree. There are scholarships available in every area of science. Professional organizations offer scholarships for STEM studies and so do many businesses. You may be able to work for a STEM business during your high school years. Some companies offer paid or unpaid internships during the summer. Once you are enrolled in college, you may be able to use that internship for college credit. Yes, you can work in a real STEM job, and it will count as class credit, too. That will enhance your résumé later.

CHAPTER TWO

Working with Biofuels

Sara Volz grew algae under her bed for her science fair project "Enhancing Algae Biofuels: Investigation of the Environmental and Enzymatic Factors Effecting Algal Lipid Synthesis," and it paid off big time. She recently won the grand prize in the Intel Science Talent Search. It came with a $100,000 scholarship. Sara was also awarded a $50,000 Davidson Fellows scholarship.

The seventeen-year-old senior from Colorado Springs, Colorado, started looking for alternatives to petroleum-based fuels in the seventh grade. She began experimenting with algae in the ninth grade. Working with algae was the "perfect fusion" of her interests in alternative energy and biochemistry.

When she was sixteen, Sara was given permission to work at the Air Force Academy's lab in Colorado Springs. Twice a week she would leave Cheyenne Mountain High School early to work on her project in the Air Force Academy's lab. For three hours every day after school she worked on her research. She grew algae in different medium formulations and catalogued the effects. "I was trying to use guided evolution, so artificial selection, to isolate populations of algae cells with abnormally high oil content," Sara told NBC News.

Sara wasn't the first to try and solve the alternative energy problem. Scientists have been attempting to find a cheap and easy way to grow these new fuels. These "biofuels" may seem simple to grow, but harvesting crops for fuel instead of food has a hidden price. The corn that is grown to make ethanol fuel is taken out of the food supply chain. With so much poverty in the world, crops diverted for use in biofuels won't feed the hungry.

The cost of producing biofuels is another obstacle to overcome. Products need to be sold at a profit, but since the fuel costs more to produce than petroleum-based fuel, consumers can't afford to buy it.

Some scientists have tried solutions such as altering the algae's genome. Others have focused on finding the optimum growing conditions for algae. Sara took a different approach. She used an herbicide that killed the algae cells with a low enzyme level. "The idea is, if you introduce this chemical, you kill everything with really low oil production," said Sara. "What you are left with is a population of cells with very high oil production."

Microbiologists study data about microscopic organisms, usually from collected samples or specimens, and look for patterns in the results.

Although she worked at the Air Force Academy's lab twice a week, the research continued at home. In glass flasks that she kept under her loft bed, Sara cultivated different types of algae. She added herbicides to the numbered flasks. These herbicides killed the algae cells that didn't produce large amounts of oil. As a result, only the algae cells that produced high quantities of oil were left.

A Microbiology Career

Studying how algae grow is the job of a microbiologist. Microbiologists study microscopic organisms such as algae, bacteria, and fungi. They analyze the growth and development of microscopic organisms.

If you want to work as a microbiologist, the minimum requirement is a bachelor's degree from an accredited college or university. Most microbiologists study microbiology or another closely related field, such as biology or biochemistry, in college.

After graduating with a bachelor's degree in microbiology, you can work in an entry-level job in a laboratory conducting scientific experiments and analyzing the results. If you want to work at a college or university, you will need to continue your studies and earn a doctorate degree, also known as a Ph.D. Earning a doctorate is required for most college and university positions. A doctorate is also required for most independent research positions.

On the Job

As a microbiologist, you will work in research and development. Just like you do now at school, you will go through all of the steps of the scientific method, the techniques used in scientific research. But at this higher professional level, your research will be much more complex. As a professional, you may also be able to initiate your own research projects.

As you work in the lab, you will identify and classify microorganisms found in different specimens collected from many sources. Depending on the study, those specimens may be from humans, food, water,

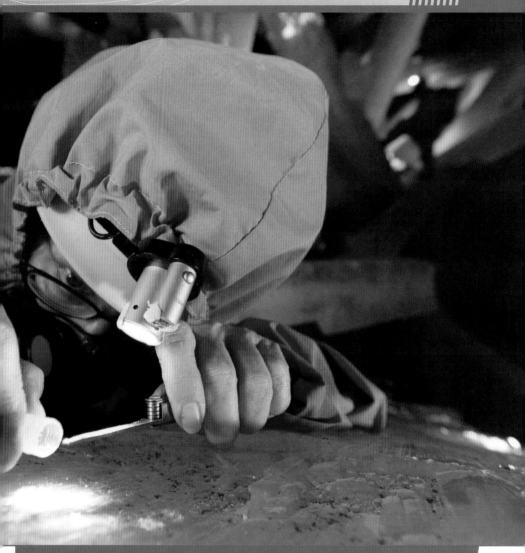

This microbiologist wears protective gear as he works in the field testing the fluid inclusions in gypsum crystals for bacteria.

and other sources. As a part of your research, you will isolate and maintain cultures of these microorganisms for future study. You may also monitor the effect of microorganisms on plants, animals, and other

THE SCIENTIFIC METHOD

1. Question formulation: Ask a scientific question.
2. Background research: Make observations as you research your question.
3. Hypothesis generation: Form a hypothesis that you can test.
4. Research design: Design an experiment to test your hypothesis.
5. Experimentation: Test your hypothesis and collect data about your progress.
6. Data analysis: Analyze your collected data and record your results.
7. Interpretation: Draw a conclusion based on your results.
8. Decision: Decide if the results agree or disagree with the hypothesis.
9. Future direction: Start over to answer the questions raised by this experiment.

microorganisms. You may even study how these microorganisms impact the environment.

After you test your hypothesis in the lab, you will analyze your data and record your results. Those results will lead you to draw a conclusion. Have you answered your research question, or do you need to go back and try another approach? To share your findings with other people at the lab, you will prepare a technical report or a research paper. At the end of this report, your conclusion will recommend the next step to take.

While you are conducting research, other researchers are working in their own labs. Just like you, they

Microbiologists identify and classify the microorganisms found in specimens from many different sources. They use laboratory instruments to conduct experiments and analyze the results.

are also writing reports about their findings. Keeping up with the findings of other researchers will also be a part of the job. You can do that by reading research reports and attending professional conferences. Sharing research is how the scientific community acquires knowledge. One idea leads to another, and that can lead to a breakthrough that benefits everyone.

You may be asked to present your research findings in a publication or at a professional event. This is where the speech classes you take in school can help you. You will have to write and present speeches to pass that class. Practice makes perfect, so you can use those skills in your job later.

The English composition classes that you have to take in school will also be invaluable. For some research positions, having your writing published on a regular basis may be required for you to keep your job. At the end of a research study, you have to write up your findings and send them to professional journals for publication.

Other scientists are not the only ones who want to know about your work. You will also need to be able to explain what you are doing to nonscientists. Reporters from the mainstream media prefer simple explanations for their audience. Knowing how to explain what you are doing in very simple language can help you reach a wider audience.

Teamwork

Today, most microbiologists work on a research team. Working across disciplines is becoming more common.

WHY BIOFUELS?

How will working with biofuels protect the environment? Let's look at what one of the major players has to say. BP is one of the world's leading international oil and gas companies, and it has employees in over eighty countries around the world. It recently released the *BP Energy Outlook 2030* report clearly stating the need for biofuels.

"By 2030, global energy consumption is projected to grow by 36 percent and, in our view, demand for liquid transport fuels will have risen by some 16 million barrels more a day. With the world's population projected to reach 8.3 billion by then, an additional 1.3 billion people will need energy. To meet this demand a diverse energy mix is needed. This is where biofuels can help; in the next two decades, biofuels are expected to provide some 20 percent (by energy) of the growth in fuel for road transport."

That means you will be working with scientists and technicians who specialize in other fields.

Someone has to oversee the team. After a few years on the job, you may find yourself supervising the work of the other team members in your lab. Or you may need to oversee the work of a multidisciplinary team. Someone needs to make sure that the work is accurate.

Although all microbiologists work with microorganisms, how their research is used can vary. As a microbiologist, you may be on a medical research team. The goal of this team is to develop new drugs to combat

These microbiologists have traveled to Antarctica to collect samples. They are working at Mount Erebus, an active volcano on Ross Island.

infectious diseases. On teams researching new drugs, microbiologists may also work with medical scientists and biochemists. A medical research team collaborates to develop vaccines, antibiotics, and other new medicines.

Microbiologists also work in medical diagnostic laboratories. If you work at a medical diagnostic laboratory, you may have physicians, nurses, and medical laboratory technologists on your team. You may also work with medical technicians and other health professionals. At a medical diagnostic laboratory, your goal is to help prevent, treat, and cure diseases.

Some microbiologists conduct basic research to increase scientific knowledge. Others take that basic research and apply it. Applied research uses information to solve problems and develop new products. This research has shown us new ways to protect the environment. One of those solutions was the development of biofuels.

On the Job in Biotech

What does a day on the job in a biotech career look like? While studying Biotechnology at Madison Area Technical College, Elizabeth Stahl worked as a laboratory intern at Valero Renewable Fuels. The Biotech Careers Web site interviewed Stahl about the work she did each day.

In the lab, Stahl performed both quality assurance (QA) and quality control (QC) testing. Quality assurance testing looks at the process that is being performed in the lab. Are the right steps being taken with the product? Quality control testing, on the other

Aviation boatswain's mate 3rd class Joshua Palomares checks the biofuel with a thermo hydrometer in the quality surveillance fuel shop aboard the aircraft carrier USS *Nimitz*.

hand, looks at the product itself. It checks to see if the product has any defects.

At Valero Renewable Fuels, Stahl worked on fermentation processes and on ethanol products and

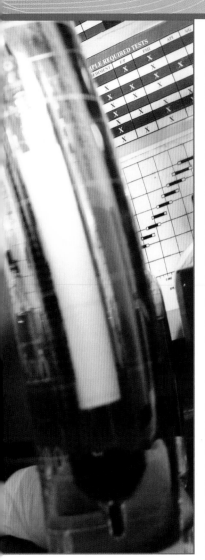

coproducts. She performed many different techniques as she tested fermentation process samples throughout the day, including checking pH level, solids testing, dextrose equivalent testing, and yeast cell counts. Samples were filtered, and an ion exchange was run every day to test for sulfate levels. The stages between fermentation and product were also tested each day. She recorded all of the test results in the computer, including the temperature of the fermentation itself.

When asked to give advice to others interested in a biotech career, Stahl said, "It is a career path with so many different outlets and opportunities to choose from. If science is of interest, biotechnology can open many different doors with careers and is also a great pre-cursor for further science education."

Those biotech careers include work as a biotech manufacturing technician or assistant, a biofuel technician, or a process development associate. You can study biotechnology at a technical college. Or you can train for a career in biofuels after completing a bachelor's or master's degree by earning a certificate.

Another Option: A Biofuels Science Certificate

At the University of California, San Diego campus, you can earn a biofuels science certificate. This is a professional certificate that is earned after a college degree. The university's Web site explains. "The Biofuels Science Specialized Certificate is aimed at training professionals for field and laboratory roles in the growing biofuels industry. It provides students hands-on technical knowledge and experience in

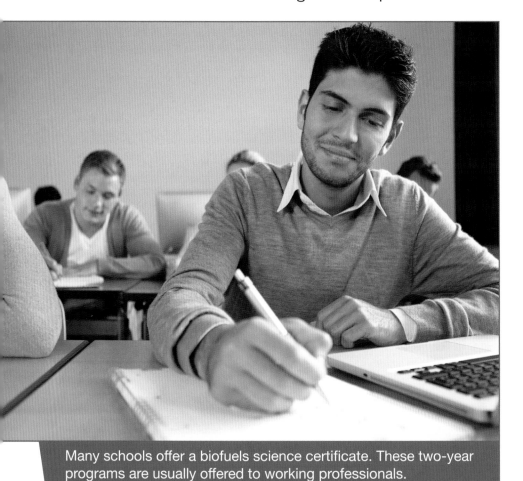

Many schools offer a biofuels science certificate. These two-year programs are usually offered to working professionals.

laboratory techniques used in biofuels production, analysis and processing."

Like any other college program there are prerequisites, or classes that you must take before you are accepted. After you are accepted into the program, you will choose from one of three specialization tracks: molecular biology, aquatic microbiology, or analytical chemistry.

Certificate programs are designed for working professionals. This two-year program is offered as a hybrid, where students can study and work at the same time. The lectures are offered online, and the lab work takes place on campus during the summer.

CHAPTER THREE

Working as an Environmental Scientist or Specialist

If you want to work to protect the environment, you can become an environmental scientist or specialist. These professionals use their knowledge of the natural sciences to protect the environment for everyone. They do this by working on both sides of today's environmental problems. First, they identify existing environmental problems. These hazards affect the health of the environment and the population. Then environmental scientists and specialists work to find solutions that minimize or eliminate existing environmental hazards.

When you work as an environmental scientist or specialist you will see all of the steps of the scientific method in action. These scientists will ask a scientific question about some aspect of the environment. They will conduct background research and generate a hypothesis that they can test. How the research is designed varies. Will a research project be the best approach? Or is an investigation needed? Perhaps a survey will be sufficient. Careful study is needed to make the best decision.

They then collect environmental data, such as samples of air, soil, water, and food. It is important to collect the samples safely, so as not to endanger the health of the scientists themselves. Safeguarding the integrity of the samples is also extremely important. All of the samples that were collected need to be analyzed. Surveys and other information collected also need to be evaluated carefully. Any threats to the environment need to be identified and assessed.

After all of the information has been gathered, a conclusion is made. A question has been asked and answered. Making a decision is the next step. Has a potential environmental problem been uncovered? If so, what steps can be taken to prevent this problem in the future? What steps are needed to control this problem? What steps are needed to fix this problem now?

Environmental plans need to be developed and put in place. That may mean working to control air pollution in the area or restoring contaminated land and water. Putting environmental plans into place requires outreach. Both the problem and ways to solve that problem need to be communicated with government officials, local businesses, and the general public.

Environmental scientists and specialists provide information and guidance on possible environmental hazards and health risks. For fellow scientists, a technical report or presentation will suffice. But for most of the population, communicating the problem and the solution in simple nontechnical language is best. The

These scientists take every precaution as they conduct tests for environmental toxins. Notice the tape sealing their shirtsleeves and pant legs.

situation must be explained clearly so everyone understands what is at stake.

Government Regulations

Every form of government (local, state, and federal) has environmental regulations of some sort. These regulations are in place so we have clean air to breathe and safe water to drink. They also limit what can be placed where, for example, so that there are no hazardous materials in the soil near our homes. Nobody wants to live in a poisonous environment.

Some regulations place limits on development near the sensitive areas of our ecosystem, such as beaches and wetlands. But environmental regulations aren't limited to sensitive areas alone. Adding a high-rise building to an already crowded urban area may impact the air quality by adding more traffic.

The water you drink is tested before, during, and after it goes through the water treatment process to ensure it meets the Environmental Protection Agency's safe drinking water standards.

The city may have regulations that require an environmental impact study before any construction can be approved.

Environmental scientists and specialists work for the government and for private industry to make sure that people comply with these regulations. The environmental scientists who work for consulting firms in private industry help their clients comply with local, state, and federal regulations.

CLEANING UP DRY CLEANING

Clean is good, but what happens when cleaning an item also makes it dirty? That was the problem that eighteen-year-old Alexa Victoria Dantzler from Manassas, Virginia, tried to solve. After reading about the toxic properties of perchloroethylene (PCE), a widely used dry cleaning chemical, she decided to study it.

Dantzler studied the levels of PCE in clothes laundered at forty-eight dry cleaning businesses in the Washington, D.C., area. She analyzed the levels of PCE residue on polyester, wool, cotton, and silk fabrics. She compared samples that had been pressed (ironed) and those that had not. She also monitored the PCE levels over time.

After dry cleaning, Dantzler discovered PCE residue on polyester, wool, and cotton fabrics, but not on silk. She also found that PCE levels dropped after a garment was pressed. The PCE levels present in the dry cleaned clothing dropped 50 percent after a week.

The wide sampling allowed Dantzler to compare the PCE levels generated at different dry cleaning businesses. She discovered that the levels varied from business to business, suggesting that different cleaning methods may influence the amount of PCE residue. For this science project, Dantzler was named an Intel Science Talent Search finalist in the chemistry category.

The federal government has a three-step evaluation process for analyzing the environmental effects of a federal project. The first step is to determine if the

Julie Masura, a researcher with the University of Washington–Tacoma environmental science program, empties a collection filter from the Thea Foss Waterway.

project will have any environmental impact. There is a list of criteria for projects that have previously been determined as having no significant environmental impact. If those match the criteria for the proposed project, all study will stop. The project will be "categorically excluded" from environmental evaluation under National Environmental Policy Act (NEPA) regulations.

If the project is not categorically excluded, it goes to step two. The federal agency that is working on the proposed project prepares a written environmental assessment (EA). This assessment will determine whether or not this new federal project would significantly affect the environment. If the answer is no, the agency issues a "finding of no significant impact" or FONSI.

On the other hand, if the answer is yes, the project moves to step three. If the federal project could have a significant impact on the environment, a new study is made. An environmental impact study (EIS) is the next step. This EIS is a detailed evaluation of the proposed project and the alternatives.

A project that may have a significant impact on the environment often requires the involvement of people outside the agency. This feedback can be given by the public and the staff at other federal agencies. Interested parties, such as environmental groups, may also get involved in the preparation of an EIS. The feedback from people outside the project may continue after a draft of the EIS is completed. When the EIS is finalized, the federal agency will prepare a public record of its decision. (These are your tax dollars at work, after all.) That public record will address how the EIS was prepared and mention the alternatives that were considered.

Although there are three distinct steps of study and decision making, some projects skip the first two. Environmentally controversial projects usually begin with step three, an environmental impact study. Projects that will have a significant impact on the environment often begin with an EIS as well.

The EIS will have a discussion of the need for action by the agency. It will discuss the purpose of the project and talk about all of the alternatives that were considered. The affected environment and the environmental consequences of the proposed action will be explained in great detail. Everyone who worked on the EIS (or was sent a copy) will be named in the document. This includes preparers, agencies, and organizations.

The federal agency that oversees all environmental issues is the Environmental Protection Agency (EPA). You can see what the EPA is working on now by visiting the Environmental Impact Statement Database

At the EPA website (www.epa.gov) you can find out what is happening in your area. Just click on the map or type in your ZIP code.

online. There you can see all EISs filed with the EPA since 2004. You can also read and comment on any EIS drafts during their forty-five-day public comment period. (A copy of each comment letter is also available in the searchable database.)

EPA inspectors are tasked with visiting workplaces to check that businesses are meeting all safety standards.

There are also environmental issues agencies at the state and local level. Every agency needs environmental scientists and specialists. To find an entry-level job as an environmental scientist or specialist,

you need a bachelor's degree in environmental science or another natural science, such as biology, chemistry, or geosciences. If you want to move up to an advanced position, you may need a master's degree. For some research positions (and for teaching college), a doctoral degree is required.

Clean Air for Everyone

You don't have to wait until you graduate from college to start helping the environment. Inspired by her family's respiratory disorders, Naomi Chetan Shah studied the impact of indoor air quality on the lung health of asthmatic patients. The seventeen-year-old from Portland, Oregon, was a recent Intel Science Talent Search finalist in the environmental science category.

Naomi worked on the project for two years, collecting more than four million indoor air quality and lung function measurements of healthy and asthmatic volunteers at work and at home. To analyze her samples, she developed a mathematical model and an interactive software application.

President Barack Obama meets with the recent Intel Science Talent Search finalists in Washington, D.C.

But she didn't stop there. Naomi also worked on a solution to the problem. She invented a biofilter that breaks down volatile organic compounds before they enter the indoor air supply. Naomi's next step is to patent both her software model and the biofilter.

CHAPTER FOUR

A Career as a Hydrologist

Too much rain or not enough? The amount of precipitation that falls in a region over time affects the lives of everyone who lives there. The scientists who study water and the water cycle are called hydrologists. They use their expertise to solve problems involving water availability or water quality. They track water distribution patterns throughout the year and analyze how these patterns influence the surrounding environment.

Most hydrologists specialize in a specific water source. Groundwater hydrologists study the water below the earth's surface. Surface water hydrologists study the water on the surface aboveground, like streams, lakes, and snow packs. Hydrometeorologists study the relationship between surface waters and water in the atmosphere.

All of these hydrologists use the scientific method to do their work. The type of

Before Superstorm Sandy in 2012, the U.S. Geological Survey placed thirty-one storm surge sensors at locations from Georgia to Maine. These sensors recorded water levels every thirty seconds.

scientific questions they ask will vary by their specialty. Each water source can be used for different purposes.

Different Types of Hydrologists

Groundwater hydrologists are often asked to find the best place to dig a well. The question that immediately follows is how much water can be pumped from that location. Groundwater hydrologists are also asked to find safe locations to build waste disposal sites. Here their expertise is needed to ensure that the waste does not seep into the ground and contaminate the groundwater.

A groundwater hydrologist may also be called a hydrogeologist. According to the Geological Society of America, "Hydrogeology is that branch of the geological sciences that is concerned with the character, source, occurrence, movement, availability, and use of

University of Nebraska assistant professor Dr. Carrick Detweiler examines a water-collecting drone at a testing site in Lincoln, Nebraska.

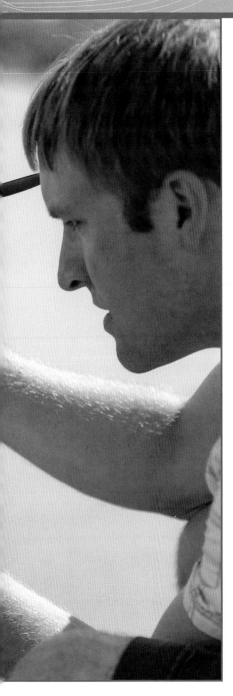

water." This professional organization has its own division just for hydrogeologists.

Surface water hydrologists are asked each year to predict future water levels. This can help people manage floods. These scientists use computer models to study weather patterns and create flood forecasts. They also help develop flood management plans. The announcement of the results of their data is released each spring during National Flood Awareness Week. Surface water hydrologists also help predict future water usage. Knowing how much water people may need in the future can help reservoir managers decide when to release or store water.

Hydrometeorologists connect the dots between the water in the atmosphere and the amount of water on the earth's surface. These scientists study how much rain or snow falls in different

ON THE JOB IN HYDROLOGY

Rebecca Bourdon works as a remediation hydrologist (or hydrogeologist) at the Minnesota Pollution Control Agency. She does technical reviews for petroleum leak sites and redevelopment properties. "In the office, we do most of our tasks on our computers," she told iSeek, a career, education, and job resource Web site in Minnesota. "We use a lot of mapping software and database programs."

Her team also conducts site visits as needed. They go to the sites to ensure that what is happening there is the same as what has been reported. "I don't see the results physically, because the work I do is below the ground and we only see change through data. But in my work, I do get to see the big-picture change, where a site that was a blighted property that the neighborhood couldn't stand is cleaned up and put to good use."

Bourdon graduated with a bachelor of science degree in geology from North Dakota State University. She is also certified as a professional geologist in the state of Minnesota, which she says was a two-part exam. "You take one part when you exit college," explained Bourdon. "And then you take the second part once you have a few years of work experience."

Bourdon explained the paradigm shift she saw in the approach to environmental remediation. Sometimes the agency will decide to go in and clean up the site and sometimes they will decide to leave the site as is. "We make decisions about leaving contamination in place where it can be left to degrade naturally through microorganisms and natural processes, and not expending extra resources for something that can take care of itself."

regions. They use this information to predict droughts. Being forewarned can help people prepare.

If you work as a hydrologist, you will collect water and soil samples for testing. You or your technician may also use remote sensing equipment to collect data. You could be asked to do research to find ways to improve water preservation and conservation. Your research can help reduce the environmental impact of pollution or erosion.

As a hydrologist, you will work closely with other professionals. How water is used affects not only people but also plants and wildlife. Depending on the project, you could work with engineers, other scientists, or public officials.

Qualifications

To work as a hydrologist, some entry-level positions require only a bachelor's degree. Most employers, however, want you to have a master's degree with a focus in the natural sciences. If you want to teach hydrology or conduct advanced research, you will need a doctorate.

In some states you will also need a license to practice. The state will ask you to verify your education. It may also ask that you have a certain level of on-the-job experience. In Wisconsin, for example, the state requires applicants to take both a fundamentals of hydrology examination and a principles and practice of hydrology examination. You can take the fundamentals of hydrology examination during the second semester of your senior year in a hydrology or water resources bachelor's program. You can also take it if you have completed a bachelor's degree and have at least five years of experience on the job. (Your work must have been supervised by a professional state-registered hydrologist for at least one year.)

The principles and practice of hydrology examination has similar requirements, but it can only be taken after graduation. You must have completed your bachelor's degree before you are permitted to take the exam. In Wisconsin, having an advanced degree (a master's degree) can qualify as a year of job experience for this exam.

At most colleges and universities, hydrology is not a major you can study. Instead, it is a specialization offered by the geosciences, environmental science, or engineering departments. To work in this field you will need extensive math training. Because of all the data that is used in this job, a background in statistics is very important. You will also need to study physical science, computer science, and life science.

Hydrologists often use geographic information systems (GIS), remote sensing, and Global Positioning System (GPS) equipment in their work. Experience with computer modeling, data analysis, and digital mapping will prepare you to enter this job market. Out in the field you will be lugging your own equipment around. Back in the lab, you will be using your computer to analyze the data you collect. Then you will use that data to make your own computer models. Like other scientists, you need to be able to communicate your findings in a way that is easy for others to understand.

Hydrologists often use GPS technology to accurately pinpoint research locations and record data.

Always in Demand

A recent *New York Times* job column headline read, "Hiring in Hydrology Resists the Slump." What this means is that even during an economic downturn, there were still new jobs for hydrologists. Government regulations are a big reason why. In 1970, the newly formed EPA established a Water Quality Office. Safe drinking water was a government priority.

"Our firm is growing, even in this economic downturn," Scott D. Warner told the *New York Times*. At the time, Warner was the principal hydrogeologist and vice president of the environmental consulting firm AMEC (Geomatrix) in Oakland, California. The company works with municipal water districts to help them manage their water and predict their needs. According to Warner, the demand for his company's services had been strong since the 1980s.

The Clean Air Act, passed in 1970 (and updated several times over the years), also affects water quality. Air pollution falls to the ground in what is known as acid rain. The nitric and sulfuric acids formed by air pollution travel in the wind far from their original sources. Acid rain can be wet or dry when it falls. If the weather is dry, the chemicals in acid rain travel as smoke or dust. In wet weather those chemicals come down as rain, fog, or snow.

Wet or dry, these acids fall to the ground and enter the water supply. Acid rain falls onto aquatic habitats. It falls into bodies of water all over the planet. Increasing the acidity of the water supply causes problems for fish and wildlife. It is toxic for some species of fish,

Factory emissions from an industrial site can affect people living hundreds of miles away. Air pollution impacts every part of the environment.

causing them to die out completely in some bodies of water. Other species that rely on those fish as a food source will be harmed by the lack of biodiversity. Acid rain also damages plants. When combined with other environmental stressors, it can slow the growth of forests or cause them to die out completely. Acid rain can change the soil, making it harder for plants to grow.

Another law affecting hydrologists was the Comprehensive Environmental Response, Compensation, and

Today scientists working in the lab use many complex tools to do their job. These sophisticated instruments help technicians find things that are otherwise invisible.

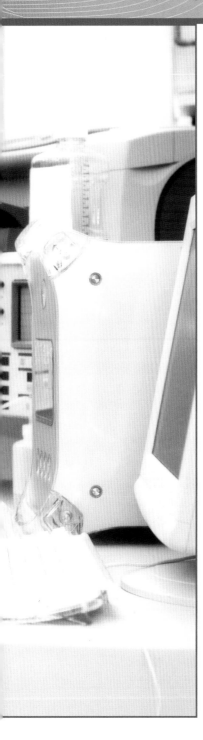

Liability Act of 1980. This environmental program, also called Superfund, was established to address abandoned hazardous waste sites.

The Clean Water Act led to the development of a list of criteria for water quality that accurately reflected the latest scientific knowledge. Criteria were developed for the protection of aquatic life as well as for human health. When you work as a hydrologist, these criteria will guide your work.

Aquatic life criteria focus on the chemical concentration goals that protect surface water for aquatic life. The biological condition of aquatic communities and the numbers and kinds of organisms present in the surface waters is another criterion. The EPA also has nutrient criteria to prevent the overenrichment of surface waters.

The human health criteria focus on drinking water and surface water. There are specific criteria for microbials, the pathogens that can be found in ground and surface waters, food sources, and drinking water. Recreational criteria protect people from exposure to pathogens as they swim and play in coastal recreational waters.

Working as a Water Quality Technician

One entry-level job to consider is water quality technician. Most employers prefer applicants that have a bachelor's degree. One to two years of laboratory experience may also be required.

A water quality technician's job is to test for microbes and chemical contaminants in recreational, potable, and waste water to determine if the water meets EPA standards. Water quality technicians also use the scientific method to compile and analyze data. They document all test results and prepare reports about their findings.

Environmental Health and Safety Technicians

If you have a two year associate's degree, an entry-level position as an environmental health and safety technician may be a good fit for you. As an environmental health and safety technician, you are responsible for maintaining a healthy work environment. To do that, you will monitor the quality of the water and the air by collecting and analyzing data. Making records of all your findings is an important part of the job. You will also be responsible for installing, calibrating, and maintaining your equipment.

CHAPTER FIVE

Helping to Feed the Planet

As a scientist, you can help feed the planet. At a recent Intel International Science and Engineering Fair (ISEF), three students from G.W. Hewlett High School in Long Island, New York, won first place in plant science and best in category. They also won the Philip V. Streich Memorial Award, which enables them to attend the London International Youth Science Forum. This two-week program is held annually for three hundred young scientists from more than fifty nations.

Samantha DiSalvo, Ryan Kenny, and Amy Vitha worked on a project titled "The Characterization of the LPS-Induced Hypersensitive Response in *Ceratopteris richardii*." Samantha, Ryan, and Amy researched how plants respond to, and sometimes resist, bacterial infections. The students said that these processes haven't previously been studied in detail at the molecular level. Working together at their high school under the mentorship of Dr. Terrence

Agricultural and food scientists are responsible in part for making sure the food we eat is safe.

Bissoondial, they developed a model to study how parts of bacteria could induce cell death in plants. This research could lead to development of plants with greater resistance to bacterial pathogens.

Agricultural and Food Scientists

If helping to feed the world appeals to you as a career, consider a job as an agricultural or food scientist. These scientists do research to ensure agricultural productivity and food safety. As an agricultural or food scientist, you could conduct research at a university, in private industry, or for the federal government. You would work in an office, in a laboratory, and out in the field.

As an agricultural or food scientist, you would play an important role in the world's food supply by working in basic or applied research and development. Basic agricultural and food research examines the biological and chemical processes of crop and livestock growth. The goal of applied research is to use basic agricultural and food research to improve these products.

Agricultural and food scientists often lead their own teams of technicians and student researchers. You could begin work on one of these teams as a student with the goal of heading up your own team after completing your studies. In some positions, the

Food scientist Dan Berg creates an omelet in one of the food kitchens at the Tate & Lyle research center in Decatur, Illinois.

employer allows the head of a research team to decide what will be researched and how that research will be conducted. There is very little direct supervision.

In this position, you may conduct research about field crops and animal nutrition. You could develop ways to improve the quantity and quality of those field crops and farm animals. You may be asked to create new food products or to develop improved food processing, packaging, or delivery methods. Or you could start by studying soil composition and plant growth.

You will work through all of the steps of the scientific method in this job. You begin with a question and then design an experiment to test your hypothesis. After you analyze your collected data and draw a conclusion based on your results, you will need to communicate your findings to the scientific community, food producers, and the public.

Many Career Paths

There are many different ways you can work in the agricultural and food science field. If you like to work with animals you may want to consider a career as an animal scientist. Animal scientists conduct research on domestic farm animals with a focus on food production. They study the genetics, nutrition, reproduction, diseases, growth, and development of farm animals. This may include crossbreeding animals to get new combinations of desirable characteristics. Animal scientists also advise farmers.

If the food served at the table interests you, a career as a food scientist or technologist may be

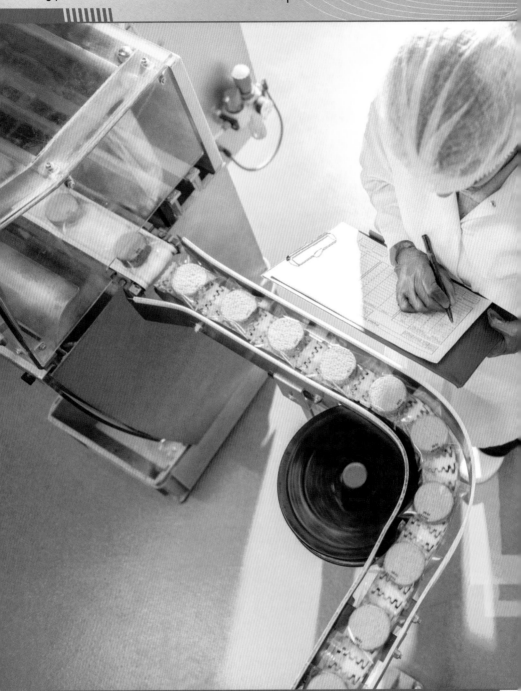

Food products are quality tested at every step of the manufacturing process. How food products are packaged can affect how they taste.

right for you. Food scientists and technologists study the nutritional content of food that comes from animals and plants. They use chemistry to research ways to make processed foods safe and healthy. They also look for new food sources. As a food technologist you would work on developing new food products.

Food safety is always a priority. Some food scientists are using nanotechnology to develop sensors that can detect contaminants. Other food scientists go out into the field and work as safety inspectors. The work that these food scientists do protects the health and safety of consumers everywhere.

Soil scientists research the composition of soil in different areas. They study how the soil affects plant growth in the area. They also investigate alternative soil treatment practices. Soil scientists advise farmers and foresters about crop productivity and soil management.

Plant scientists also work with farmers to improve crop productivity. But a plant scientist focuses on the plant itself, not the soil it grows in. Controlling pests and weeds safely is also an important focus of their work.

Education

How much education you need to work in this field depends on where you want to work. Most agricultural and food scientists have a bachelor's degree. This degree allows them to work in private industry for food production companies, farms, and processing plants. A bachelor's degree may also be sufficient for working on research at a pharmaceutical company. For a university research position, however, a doctoral degree is usually required. This is also the case if you want to work with animals. Many animal scientists earn a doctorate of veterinary medicine (DVM). Some also earn a Ph.D.

When you go to college you may want to select agricultural science as your major. As an undergraduate you will study biology, chemistry, botany, and plant conservation. If you want to be a food scientist, look for a school where you can take food chemistry, food analysis, food microbiology, food engineering, and food processing operations courses. If you want to be a soil and plant scientist, courses in plant pathology, soil chemistry, entomology, plant physiology, and biochemistry will help you on your career path.

Certification

For some careers, a professional certificate is another way to show your expertise. If you work with soils, you can be certified by the Soil Science Society of America (SSSA). To become a certified professional soil scientist, you need both a college degree and on-the-job

Quality control microbiologist Kim Egger inspects a bacteria culture taken from ground meat processed at Excel Corporation's slaughterhouse in Schuyler, Nebraska.

experience. You must pass both the Fundamentals of Soils Science Examination and the Professional Practice of Soil Science Examination. These exams are administered twice a year, and some states require them for state licensing purposes.

The Soil Science Society of America (SSSA) also offers an agronomy certification. (Agronomy is the science of soil management and the production of field crops.) To earn this certificate, you will need to pass the International Certified Crop Adviser (ICCA) Exam

AGRICULTURAL OR FOOD SCIENCE TECHNICIAN

If studying for an advanced degree is not something you can do right now, you may be able to find work as an agricultural or food science technician. While you are still in high school, you should take as many high school science and math classes as you can. To work as a technician, you will need a solid background in applied chemistry, physics, and math.

The next step is to go to school for an associate's degree in animal science or a related field from an accredited college or university. A background in the biological sciences is crucial for food and agricultural technicians. Study biology, chemistry, animal science, and agricultural engineering. Keep your eye out for other opportunities as well. Your school may offer internships, cooperative education, and other experiential programs. These on-the-job training programs can lead to a full-time job after you graduate.

You will work under the supervision of an experienced technician or a scientist. Your job will be to measure and analyze the quality of food and agricultural products. Agricultural technicians in private industry test crops and animals for disease. Food science technicians in private industry inspect crops, animals, and processed food. They test anything that can be eaten by a consumer to make sure that it is safe. They also check to make sure that the product is what it says on the label.

Agricultural and food science technicians who work for the federal government are tasked with monitoring the food supply. Their job is to make sure that the law is followed. The FDA Food Safety Modernization Act was passed in 2011 and it is still being updated to reflect a change in focus from responding to food contamination to preventing it. As a result, the frequency of food inspections has increased and performance standards have been raised.

On the Food and Drug Administration (FDA) Web site, FDA commissioner Margaret A. Hamburg explains, "Preventing problems before they cause harm is not only common sense, it is the key to food safety in the 21st century. We cannot afford to wait until people become ill to realize there is a problem." As an agricultural and food science technician, you will be on the front lines of the battle for food safety.

and the local board exam for your state or province. You must have experience in the field before taking this exam

If you work as an animal scientist, you can be certified by the American Registry of Professional Animal Scientists (ARPAS). To register as an associate member of ARPAS, you must have a B.S., M.S., or Ph.D. in one of the animal sciences (or a closely related field). If you are studying for an advanced degree, you can apply for a graduate student membership.

To become a member of ARPAS you will be asked to pass an exam in your area of specialization.

ARPAS has thirteen categories: aquaculture, beef cattle, companion animals, dairy cattle, goats, horses, laboratory animals, poultry, sheep, swine, dairy product science, meat science, and poultry products. (An exam is required for each area of specialization that you select.)

As a member of ARPAS, you can qualify to be board certified by the American College of Animal Sciences (ACAS). The ACAS offers board certification in applied animal behavior sciences (animal husbandry), animal food science (meat, poultry meat, milk, and eggs), animal genetics, animal nutrition, animal physiology, and animal welfare science.

Board certification is the highest level of certification for these

In Peru, Professor David Spooner, researcher at the University of Wisconsin, holds a little tuber of a plant known as the predecessor of the domestic or cultivated potato.

disciplines. It is valued both by employers and by clients. Being certified at this level verifies your expertise in a specific discipline of animal science.

On the Job with a Botanist

"Ever since I could remember all I ever wanted to be was a botanist," says David Spooner, research botanist with the USDA Agricultural Research Service in the Vegetable Crops Research Unit in Madison, Wisconsin, in an interview on the Botanical Society of America Web site. "As a child I pretty much lived in the various woods near our home in southwestern Ohio, and knew every trail and creek bed by heart. I was always curious about what the plants were called." Spooner teaches at the University of Wisconsin and conducts research with his team. He writes papers and seeks funding through grants while his USDA lab technician and graduate students perform both lab and field work. "This truly is a dream job," says Spooner. "The USDA hires and retains scientists to be leaders in their research areas, and productive scientists are given freedom to direct their own programs within the context of their job assignment."

Spooner's specialty is wild and cultivated potatoes. In his research, he has discovered almost thirty species that grow in North and Central America. There are about 150 species in South America. "My USDA job assignment is to collect these species on yearly expeditions of two months each throughout the Americas," says Spooner. "How cool is that? I then use these collections to study their species boundaries and relationships with modern morphological and molecular methods, such as marker data (as AFLPs), and DNA sequences of chloroplast and single-copy nuclear genes." This research is important because "the wild and native cultivated species have resistances to many of the diseases and pests that plague" potatoes that are planted domestically.

CHAPTER SIX

Working in the World of Genetics

A t a recent Intel ISEF, seventeen-year-old Hannah Wastyk of Palmyra, Pennsylvania, won $5,000 for placing first in the cellular and molecular biology category. For her ISEF project, Hannah worked with Penn State Hershey College of Medicine researchers on gene inhibitors for melanoma. She developed a treatment for melanoma that killed a large proportion of cancer cells but didn't affect most healthy cells.

Hannah also received the Dudley R. Herschbach Stockholm International Youth Science Seminar Award. As a part of that award, Hannah was able to travel to Stockholm, Sweden, for a week to attend the Nobel Prize ceremonies. (Herschbach won the Nobel Prize in Chemistry in 1986. He is also the former chairman of Society for Science and the Public, the organization that has run ISEF since it began in 1950.)

Biochemists and Biophysicists

If finding out more about cell development, growth, and heredity appeals to you, a career as a biochemist or a biophysicist might be in your future. These scientists study the chemical and physical principles of living things. By researching biological processes, biochemists and biophysicists play a key role in developing new medicines to fight disease.

To work as a biochemist or biophysicist, you will need to earn a doctoral degree, also known as a Ph.D. When you begin college, you can study for a bachelor's degree in biochemistry or a related field, such as biology, chemistry, physics, or engineering. (Many schools have bachelor's degree programs in biochemistry, but schools that offer a bachelor's degree program in biophysics are few and far between.)

As an undergraduate, you will take courses in biology, chemistry, and physics. Because of the complex data analysis that is required on the job, you will also need to take courses in mathematics and computer science. Working in the laboratory is also a requirement in most bachelor's degree programs.

Your laboratory coursework is the best way to prepare for a career in this field. Be sure to look for internship possibilities while you are in college. You may be able to work in the lab of a pharmaceutical or medicine manufacturer. This valuable work experience can help you find an entry-level position in the industry after graduation with a bachelor's degree. Or you can use this experience to help prepare you for graduate school. If you want to become the lead researcher

The laboratory work you conduct at school can lead you to a career in genetics. There are exciting discoveries to be made in this field.

(also known as the principal investigator) you will need to earn a Ph.D.

Most Ph.D. programs have two years of advanced coursework in topics such as toxicology, genetics, and proteomics (the study of proteins). As a graduate student, you will spend a lot of time in the laboratory conducting research. As a result, it usually takes four to six years to earn a doctoral degree in biochemistry or biophysics.

After earning a Ph.D., most biochemistry and biophysics graduates work in a temporary postdoctoral research position for several years. This is commonly called a postdoc. The research that you perform in your postdoctoral position can help you get a job as a PI, a principal investigator.

If you want to work as the principal investigator, it is essential to have your research published while you are doing postdoctoral work. Writing for a publication about your postdoctoral work gives employers clear and visible evidence of the research that you have done. This is especially true for individuals who want to work on the faculty of a college or university.

Biochemists and biophysicists plan and conduct complex projects in both basic and applied research. In basic research you will work to discover what has previously been unknown. In applied research you will try to find ways to use what you have discovered in everyday life.

In the lab, as an undergraduate, a graduate student, a postdoc, or the principal investigator, you will work as part of a team. Your team will use electron microscopes, lasers, and other laboratory equipment to carry out their research.

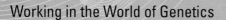

It's important to share your findings with your team. Talking things over can help you formulate the questions you need to take your research to the next level.

Your team may isolate, analyze, and synthesize proteins, enzymes, DNA, and other molecules. They might research the effects of substances such as drugs, hormones, and food on tissues and biological processes. On the job, your team may also work with experts in other fields, such as physics, chemistry, computer science, and engineering.

Biochemists and biophysicists who conduct basic research have their projects paid for by outside sources. To obtain the funding they need, the scientists must submit written grant proposals to various sources to pay for work they do on their research projects. Colleges and universities fund some research grants. Private foundations and even the federal government pay for basic research to be performed.

To continue to have their research project funded, the team will need to share their findings with their benefactors. In technical reports or research papers, they will keep their colleagues informed. Many teams will also share their work with the scientific community at large. That may mean writing for publication or presenting the findings at a professional conference, or both.

After the basic research is published, it is up to the applied researchers to find ways to use that information to help others. Biochemists and biophysicists have used applied research to develop tests to detect diseases, genetic disorders, and other illnesses. They have taken basic research and applied it to develop new drugs and medications.

Applied research in biochemistry and biophysics has also been used in agriculture to develop alternative

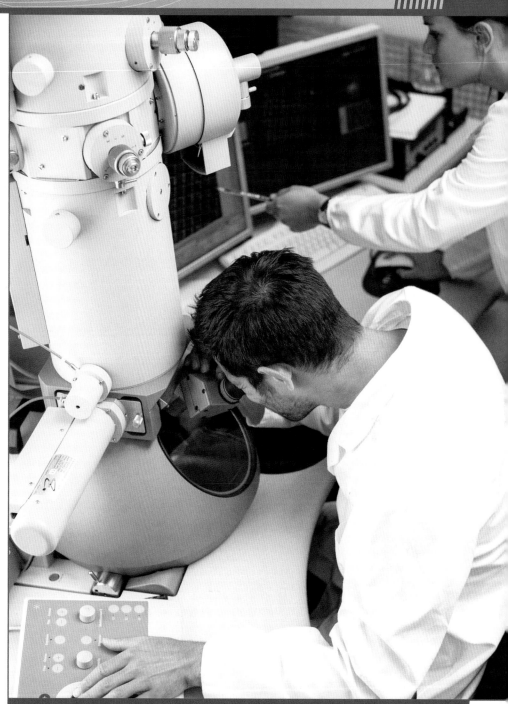

The microscopes you use in college may be much more advanced than the ones you are using in high school. Some use lasers or electrons to illuminate the image.

WHO OWNS YOUR GENES?

Genetic testing is one way to help fight inherited diseases. The only way to find out if you have inherited a mutated gene is to test for it. To do that, you go to a lab and pay a fee. But what happens when the lab insists that it owns your genes, and it wants you to pay more than $3,000 to be tested for a single gene?

Who owns your genes anyway? The obvious answer would be you because they come from your body. But that's not what happened as scientific research progressed. Companies that isolated human genes in the laboratory filed patents for them. If you wanted to be tested for these patented genes you had to pay the company that held the patent. That's what Myriad Genetics, a company in Utah, wanted. The company filed patent infringement suits against other labs that were testing for the gene that Myriad Genetics had isolated. The case went all the way to the United States Supreme Court.

On June 13, 2013, the Supreme Court made its ruling. Myriad Genetics lost the case in a unanimous 9–0 decision. Speaking for the Court, Justice Clarence Thomas said, "We hold that a naturally occurring DNA segment is a product of nature and not patent-eligible merely because it has been isolated."

The Los Angeles Times said, "The 9–0 ruling is likely to be welcomed by medical researchers across the nation who have wanted more freedom to experiment with treatments using genetic material." The New York Times reported, "The court's ruling will also shape the course of scientific research and medical testing in other fields, and it may alter the willingness of businesses to invest in the expensive work of isolating and understanding genetic material." Only time will tell.

fuels, such as biofuels. Producing fuel from plants, a renewable energy source, is one way to protect the environment. Genetically engineered crops are another product of applied research by biochemists. The goal was to make these crops more resistant to drought, disease, insects, and other afflictions.

In a recent census, 44 percent of all biochemists and biophysicists did research and development in the physical, engineering, and life sciences. Twenty-two percent worked in pharmaceutical and medicine manufacturing. Only 14 percent worked in education (colleges, universities, and professional schools).

Biological Technicians

After graduating from college with a bachelor's degree in biology, you can begin a career as a biological technician. You can use your laboratory experience from college and turn it into a full-time job. As a biological technician, you will work in a laboratory conducting tests and experiments for biological or medical scientists.

On the job, you will be responsible for laboratory instruments and equipment, such as microscopes, scales, and test tubes. It will be your job to set them up and keep them clean. You will also be responsible for gathering and preparing the samples tested in the lab. These samples may include blood, food, or bacteria cultures.

In addition to all of the preparation work, you will also be responsible for conducting biological tests and experiments. Just as you did in college, you will be asked to follow all of the steps of the scientific method. Collecting data will mean carefully documenting your work before analyzing it and interpreting the results. As always, you will summarize your findings in a written report.

As a biological technician, you will work on a research team. On most teams, the technician is responsible for conducting the scientific tests or experiments. The biological technician also analyzes the data for the team. Your work, of course, will be done under the supervision of a biologist or another scientist.

One example of a biological technician is a genomics technician. As a genomics technician, you would use different technologies to determine and then compare DNA and RNA sequences. First, you would need to isolate RNA and DNA from samples. Then you could construct libraries, perform quality control, and carry out titrations. On the job as a genomics technician, you would work with a variety of sequencing technologies.

Some companies will hire you to work as a genomics technician with a two-year associate's degree, while others require a bachelor's degree in biology. If you want to work as a genomics technician, spend time in the molecular biology lab working with RNA and DNA during college. (Some genomics companies want to see two years of lab experience in their specialty before they hire you.)

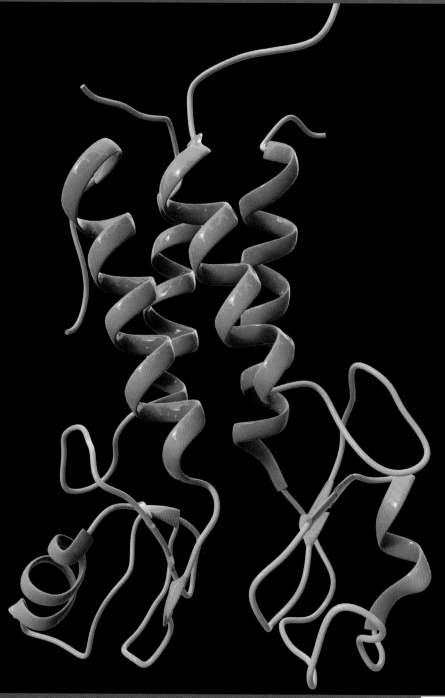

This is a molecular model of the breast cancer type 1 susceptibility (*BRCA1*) protein. Mutations in the *BRCA1* protein can prevent it from repairing damaged DNA.

As you can see from the genomics tech example, it is very important to have laboratory experience when applying for a job as a biological technician. Most biological technicians who are hired list their laboratory experience during college on their job application. While you are still in school, take biology courses that require laboratory work. Look for a summer internship at a pharmaceutical and medicine manufacturer that can give you laboratory experience. Employers want you to know what you are doing before they hire you.

Bioinformatics and Genomics

Jonah Kallenbach, a high school senior at Germantown Academy in Fort Washington, Pennsylvania, won second place (and a $75,000 scholarship) at a recent Intel Science Talent Search. The seventeen-year-old's bioinformatics and genomics project broke new ground in predicting protein binding for drug therapy.

Jonah told NBC News that he worked in a biophysics lab in the ninth grade. In that lab he learned about bioinformatics, which is the application of computer science to other fields, including biology. "I realized the power computer science can have," said Jonah.

Jonah started working with computers to try to solve a mystery about proteins. There are two types of proteins in the molecular system of a cell—ordered and disordered. What ordered proteins did was well known. Disordered proteins, on the other hand, were a wild card. "They can fold many different ways, potentially they can form in many different ways, and potentially they can have many binding partners," Jonah told NBC News.

But no one knew how to predict the interactions between disordered regions and their binding partners. That was the question that Jonah wanted to answer. He thought that being able to predict these interactions could be the key to helping scientists find a cure for certain diseases.

Jonah built a computer program to explore those interactions. He validated his results with proteins coded by the *BRCA1* gene. (The name *BRCA1* stands for breast cancer 1, early onset. It is also called breast cancer susceptibility gene 1.) Normally, this gene on chromosome 17 acts as a tumor suppressor in the body. When this gene mutates, however, it can cause breast cancer in women and men. *BRCA1* mutations are also linked to cervical, uterine, pancreatic, and colon cancer in women as well as pancreatic, testicular, and early onset prostate cancer in men.

Jonah's work with the *BRCA1* gene may lead to a new type of drug design. Targeting the disordered regions of a print may be the next wave of drug research and development.

CHAPTER SEVEN

Better Living Through Science

Using computational analysis, seventeen-year-old Raghav Tripathi virtually screened more than a million molecules. This Westview High School student from Portland, Oregon, was trying to find molecules on anandamide, a fatty acid naturally produced in the body.

At an elevated level, anandamide has painkilling effects. However, fatty acid binding proteins degrade anandamide. Raghav searched for a way to inhibit the degradation process. The key to doing that was finding molecules that had a binding property similar to those fatty acid binding proteins.

Once Raghav found one, he synthesized an optimized compound that inhibited the fatty acid binding proteins even more. For his work on new pain relievers, Raghav came in first place in the biochemistry category of the Intel Science Talent Search. His research has also been published in several peer-reviewed journals.

Medical Scientists

If you chose a career as a medical scientist, you would plan and direct studies to investigate human diseases. In your research, you would look for ways to prevent and treat those diseases. Medical scientists often use clinical trials to research their findings. This means that they work directly with patients who have the disease they are trying to treat.

To become a medical scientist you will need to have a Ph.D. in biology or a related life science. Some medical scientists get a medical degree instead of a Ph.D. but continue to conduct research instead of practicing as physicians. It is also possible to study for a combined M.D./Ph.D. degree.

So how do you begin? Look for an accredited college or university where you can earn a bachelor's degree in a biological science. For your major, you will need to take courses in life sciences, as well as physics, chemistry, and mathematics. You will also need to take English composition and speech classes. These courses may not seem to be related to your major. However, as a medical scientist conducting independent research, you will find that they are essential.

To raise the funds needed to pay for your work as a researcher you will need to write grant proposals. You must be able to communicate clearly about what you want to do and also about what you have accomplished so far. Writing about the results of your research for publication in a journal is a task that all medical researchers do. They also give talks at staff meetings and other events such as medical conferences.

This biomedical scientist is working with samples in a diabetes clinic. Each patient's sample is carefully labeled to ensure accuracy.

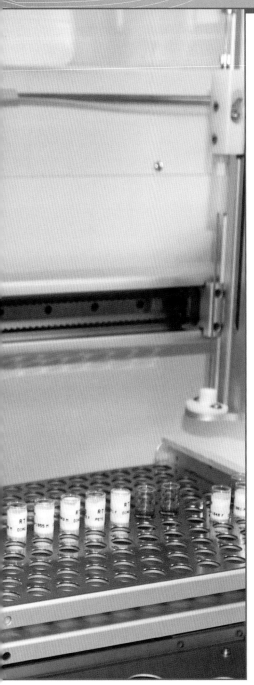

After you graduate from college with a bachelor's degree in science, the next step is to enter a graduate program. For a career as a medical scientist there are two choices. You can study for a Ph.D. or a joint M.D./ Ph.D. If you are accepted into a Ph.D. program in the biological sciences, you will have about six years of study ahead of you. You will select one field of study, such as bioinformatics, genetics, or pathology, as your specialty.

If you are accepted into a joint M.D./Ph.D. program, you will enroll at a medical college. For the next seven or eight years, you will learn how to become both a medical doctor and a research scientist. You will learn the clinical skills you need to be a physician and the research skills you need to be a scientist.

Medical Scientist Training Program

Another name for the joint M.D./Ph.D. program is the Medical Scientist Training Program (MSTP). This program was established by the federal government in 1964. It is administered by the National Institute of General Medical Sciences (NIGMS). You may have never heard of this organization, but if you want to be a scientist, it wants to support you. The NIGMS website explains that it can fund your work, and funding can start when you are a student in one of its programs. Earning a joint M.D./Ph.D. can take seven or eight years, but the agency that started the Medical Scientist Training Program can help you pay for six years in the program. How will you pay for the other years? The NIGMS website says, "All institutions identify other sources of support for a trainee's additional years of study."

The MSTP stated recently that it had 43 participating programs with a total of 932 trainees. There were also approximately 75 medical schools with M.D./Ph.D. studies that did not have NIGMS MSTP training grants. These training grants do not have to be repaid, so it is worth investigating. This program has about 170 positions for new students annually.

An MSTP program is divided into three phases. For the first two years, you will go to medical school. Most schools number these years as MS1 and MS2. At the University of Texas Southwestern, these first two years are called the MSTP pre-clinical years. The next phase is three (or more) years of graduate study. During this

National Institute of
General Medical Sciences

Basic Discoveries for Better Health

NIGMS Home | Research Funding | Research Training | News & Meetings | Science Education | About NIG

Fact Sheets
Basic biomedical research areas
and their impact on health

More Info ▶

1 2 3 4 5

Quick Links

New on This Site
Feedback Loop Blog
Biomedical Beat News Digest
Findings Magazine
Images, Videos and More
Congressional Materials
Advisory Council
Job Vacancies

unding Opportunities

GMS Funding Opportunities by Keyword(s)

Search

omedical Technology Research Resource (P41)

e-application for a Biomedical Technology
search Resource (X02)

nters of Biomedical Research Excellence
OBRE) (P20)

deling the Scientific Workforce (U01)

th L. Kirschstein National Research Service
ard (NRSA) Institutional Research Training
ant (Parent T32)

re Funding Opportunities

Latest News

Enzyme's Evolution Traced From Bacteria to Humans

Fatty Acids May Be Crucial to Embryonic
Development

Protein Needed for Normal Cell Movement May Also
Promote Cancer Metastasis

Drug-Dispensing Contact Lens Delivers Glaucoma
Medication Continuously for a Month

New Method of DNA Editing Can Uncover Cryptic
Gene Clusters

First Large-Scale Demonstration of Real-Time Flu
Forecasting System

More News

Media Resources

URL Changes
A new content management system
changed many URLs on this site; plea
update your bookmarks as needed.

Inside Life Science
A series that keeps you
informed about the
science of health

Image and Video Gallery
Searchable database
of photos, illustrations
and videos from NIGMS

E-mail Updates

Receive NIGMS e-mail updates

Enter e-mail address   Sign U

Up to top

is page last reviewed on November 22, 2013

On the NIGMS website (www.nigms.nih.gov) you can find out more
about research training programs and funding. There is also news
about the latest developments in medical science.

time you will conduct biomedical research for your dissertation and earn your Ph.D. degree. These are your MSTP Ph.D./thesis years. Then it's back to medical school for your final two years, MS3 and MS4. Now you are in your MSTP post-Ph.D. years. It's time to work on your clinical studies and earn your M.D. degree.

The United States Medical Licensing Examination

To practice as a medical doctor, you must go to medical school and pass a series of exams so you can be licensed. The first test, called Step 1, is taken after you complete the first two years of medical school. After you complete the fourth year of medical school you take the Step 2 tests. The second test is divided in two parts: clinical knowledge (Step 2CK) and clinical skills (Step 2CS).

There is a computerized United States Medical Licensing Examination test for three of

West Virginia University School of Medicine dean Arthur Ross congratulates class president Masih Ahmed after every member of the class passed the U.S. Medical Licensing Exam Step One.

the steps, Step 1, Step 2CK, and Step 3. The Step 2CS test, however, is not computerized. For the clinical skills test, you will work in a clinic with a dozen different "standardized" patients. You will gather information from these patients in person or on the telephone. For the patients that you see in person, you will also perform a limited physical examination. After each "patient encounter," you will be asked to write a patient note, just like you would for any patient's medical record.

Step 3 of the United States Medical Licensing Examination can only be taken after you graduate from medical school with your M.D. Each state has its own conditions for applicants who want to take this test. You must meet the state medical board requirements of the state you will be sitting for.

Working as a Medical Scientist

Like other scientists with doctoral degrees, medical scientists often continue their education with postdoctoral work. You may find a postdoctoral position at a university or a federal agency, like the National Institutes of Health. Conducting postdoctoral research will give you even more laboratory experience. Some postdoctoral positions later become permanent jobs.

Where can you find work as a medical scientist? In the most recent census, 56 percent of all medical scientists worked at research-based institutions. Thirty-five percent worked for scientific research and development services, while 24 percent worked for colleges, universities, and professional schools. The rest worked in pharmaceutical and medicine manufacturing

CHEMICAL TECHNICIANS

If you want to work in a lab but you don't want to go to college for years and years, a career as a chemical technician may be right for you. You only need two years of training after high school to find work as a chemical technician.

As a chemical technician, you will work in a lab assisting chemists and chemical engineers. You can work on research or help develop and produce chemical products. You are also responsible for the equipment you work with.

There are two main types of chemical technicians. Laboratory technicians help scientists conduct experiments. They prepare chemical solutions and test products for quality and performance. Processing technicians, on the other hand, monitor the quality of products and processes at chemical manufacturing facilities. They collect samples and test them for impurities. They also test product packaging.

For most chemical technician jobs you need an associate's degree in applied science or chemical technology. You can attend a technical college or a community college. Many of these institutions also offer internships and cooperative-education programs. This can help you gain work experience while you are still in school. The lab work that you conduct at school can also help you get a job.

(12 percent) and general medical and surgical hospitals (11 percent). Every one of them is working to make the world a better place with medical science.

Original Research

For his Intel Science Talent Search project in chemistry, seventeen-year-old Peter Kraft investigated the synthesis of novel coordination polymers. These polymers are massive molecules with complex network structures. They are used in the storage of hydrogen in fuel cells, gas purification, and LED lighting.

As a Munster High School student, in Munster, Indiana, Peter synthesized and characterized ten new polymers with a wide range of complexity and structural composition. This could improve methods of gas storage or increase the speed and efficacy of chemical reactions.

The fight against disease is worldwide. In Melbourne, Australia, Dr. Peter Czabotar (*left*) shows Prime Minister Tony Abbott an anticancer molecule on the screen.

Peter's original research in chemistry was awarded best in category at the ISEF. But it doesn't end there. This Indiana student's work with polymers has already been published in the *Journal of Molecular Structure* and the journal *Acta Crystallographica*.

Chemists and Materials Scientists

If a career in chemistry interests you, you may want to work as a chemist or a materials scientist. In this job, you will study the structures, compositions, reactions, and other properties of substances. Then you can use that knowledge to develop new and improved products, processes, and materials.

As a chemist or a materials scientist, you will plan and carry out complex research projects. As the head of a research team, you will direct your technicians and other workers. You may also need to instruct them on proper chemical processing and testing procedures.

In the lab, you will prepare test solutions, compounds, and reagents, substances used in chemical analysis. You will study these substances to determine both their chemical and physical properties. You may also be asked to test materials to ensure that safety and quality standards are met. At the end of your testing, you will write up the results of your findings in a technical report and present it to your colleagues.

A collaborative approach to research is becoming quite common. Most chemists and materials scientists work as part of a team. Their team members may be biologists, physicists, computer specialists, or engineers.

Chemists work in both basic and applied research. For basic research, chemists may investigate the properties, composition, or structure of matter. They would also experiment with the combination of elements and the reactions of substances to each other. The goal of applied research is to find a way to use basic research in everyday life. Chemists have developed and improved thousands of products, including drugs, plastics, and cleaners.

Materials scientists usually work in applied research. To develop new products or improve existing ones, they study the structures and chemical properties of different materials. They work to find ways to develop new materials for products. This may mean strengthening old materials or combining different materials in a new way. It is because of materials scientists that we have metallic alloys and superconducting materials.

In the lab, chemists and materials scientists use computers and sophisticated laboratory instruments. To do their work, these scientists use modeling, simulation, and experimental analysis. This may include three-dimensional (3D) computer modeling software.

Many chemists specialize in one branch of the field. You may want to work as an analytical chemist. These scientists analyze the structure, composition, and nature of substances. They study the relationships and interactions between the different parts of compounds. Their research is used in such things as pollution control, pharmaceuticals, and food safety.

Organic chemists study molecules that contain carbon. This study helps them make new organic substances that are used in commercial products, like pharmaceutical drugs and plastics.

Inorganic chemists work with materials, like metals, that do not contain carbon. They study the structure, properties, and reactions of molecules to see how these materials can be modified, separated, or used in products. Inorganic substances are used in superconductors and ceramics.

Physical chemists study how matter behaves at the molecular and atomic level. They research how chemical reactions occur. This will help them see how complex structures are formed. Physical chemists and materials scientists often work together to develop potential uses for new materials.

Medicinal chemists work on teams to create and test new drug products. They research and develop chemical compounds for pharmaceutical drugs. Medicinal chemists also use applied research to help manufacturers produce new drugs on a large scale.

What to Study in College

As an undergraduate, you will study all areas of chemistry: analytic, organic, inorganic, and physical. You may be able to find an entry-level job with a bachelor's degree. However, if you want to conduct research, you will need a master's or a doctoral degree. As a graduate student you can specialize in one area of chemistry, such as physical or analytic chemistry. Students who specialize in organic or medicinal chemistry can work in a pharmaceutical career later on.

Not every school offers a degree in materials science, so you may want to major in chemistry, physics, or engineering. You can also study to become a materials scientist in the university's engineering department. Check the school website to see if the engineering school offers a joint degree in materials science and engineering.

CHAPTER EIGHT

The Future of STEM Careers in Science

After all of your schooling, how will you get you first job as a scientist? The first thing to understand is that finding a job is about a different kind of chemistry than the type you may be studying in school. When you apply for a job in any profession, personal chemistry is very important. Getting a job isn't just about your skills. It's also about how you get along with the people who are doing the hiring.

You've studied for all of the many tests you've had in school. You'll need to use the same approach to job hunting. Instead of satisfying a teacher, now you have a potential employer to impress. To get what you want (a great job) you'll have to give that employer what he or she wants. The best way to do that is to study and practice. Study what the job market asks for and what other job applicants do. And make time to practice. Like every new skill, getting a new job takes time to master. Write

WHAT DO EMPLOYERS WANT?

"Who are the scientists that industry wants to hire?" asked William Banholzer, chief technology officer and an executive vice president of Dow Chemical Company in Midland, Michigan. In a recent issue of *Science Careers* magazine, he also provided the answer. The scientists that industry wants to hire are "brilliant people who are creative and curious and can communicate."

In the article "How to Succeed in Industry by Really Trying" Banholzer said, "you'd better be able to be very effective communicating with your fellow scientists, but you'd better also be able to understand your audience. The less technically astute your audience is, the better you should be at communication."

"If you and I do great science, but you also took some business classes and communication," said Banholzer, "you're more employable." So spend time in the lab during school, but also make time for other studies. Learning how to work with others can help you in school now and on the job later.

up your résumé or CV several different ways. Ask a friend to interview you so you can practice and sound like you know what you're talking about on the big day of the interview. Practice, practice, practice.

Job Boards

The first place to look for a position is on a job board. Check the listings at your school first. If an employer has taken the time to ask the school to list a job, that

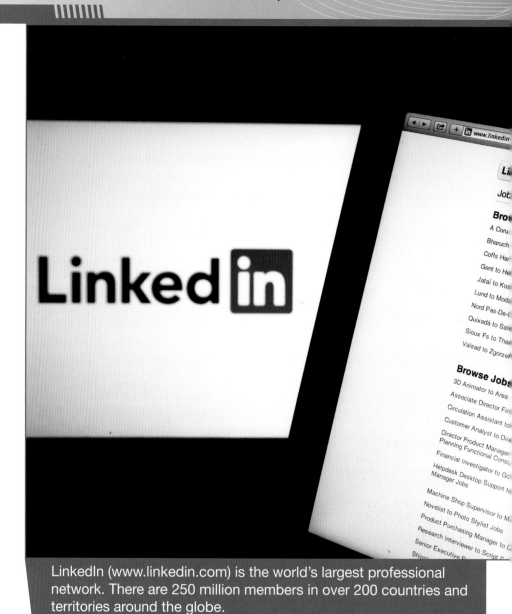

LinkedIn (www.linkedin.com) is the world's largest professional network. There are 250 million members in over 200 countries and territories around the globe.

means they are looking for students like you. Use that to your advantage.

There are lots of job boards online that you can check. You can review the boards that everyone uses,

such as Monster and LinkedIn. But go deeper and search the science job boards, too. The jobs listed at TheLabRat .com, ScienceCareers.org, EdsJobList.com, and New-ScientistJobs.com are all going to be science oriented. You won't need to wade through pages of unrelated jobs to find what you want.

Your Résumé

To help employers (and recruiters) find you, set up a free account on LinkedIn. Some recruiters use keyword searches to find people for the companies they work for. Look at the LinkedIn accounts of other students to see how they have talked about their experience. What keywords did they use? Visit the LinkedIn résumé pages of people who have a job like the one you want. Study how they worded their résumé listings and learn from those examples.

If you plan to stay in the academic world, you may need to prepare a CV, a curriculum vitae, or just "vita." A CV is much longer than a single-page résumé. It allows you to go into detail about both your academic and research experience. There is no standard format for a CV, so you will need to look at other vitas in your specialty as you prepare yours.

When you find a job listing that you can reply to, follow up right away. Send in a résumé exactly the way the company has requested it. Don't give the person handling the applications a reason to eliminate you from the running. Follow directions precisely. That may mean that you have to customize your résumé to meet the company's requirements. Just make sure that it all fits on one page. If it's any longer it may be automatically rejected.

If you are given the opportunity to send in a cover letter with your résumé, customize that, too. Look at the language that is used on the company's website, and use it in your letter. Every workplace has it own culture, its own language. What is the company's mission statement? What values

When you go for a job interview, you can expect to meet with many different people. Be calm and listen carefully before you answer their questions.

does it talk about? If you can, use the terminology that the company uses when you talk to its representatives. That will let them know that you will fit into their culture.

The Interview

A job interview is usually a long process with many steps. The first task is sending in your résumé. Before a potential employer ever meets you, the words on your résumé do the talking. This is why it is so important to work through several drafts of your résumé to make it as strong as it can be. Ask a friend to help you. Have someone else read it and make suggestions. Then rewrite it and ask for another edit.

Many employers will set up a phone interview as the second step. Just like the résumé step, the phone interview step is designed to eliminate as many candidates as possible. Good phone manners are extremely important. Take the call in a quiet place and give it your full attention.

If you pass the phone interview, you may be called in for a face-to-face interview. Now it's not just what you say; it's what you look like, too. On the day of the interview, make sure that you look professional. Dress like others at the place

Remember that prospective employers want you to have a successful interview. After all, they are conducting these interviews because they are looking for someone to hire!

of employment do. You want to look like you already work there.

Before the big day, practice answering possible interview questions with a friend. You can take turns being the employer and the interviewee. By role-playing, you can think through what you really want to say. You'll give yourself time to think of that great answer now. (After the real interview is over, it's too late to change your answer.)

At many places of employment, there will be a series of face-to-face interviews. Being invited back several times to meet different individuals in the company is the norm. Each time you are invited back means that you are one step closer to being the person who is hired for the job.

Each interview will also give you a better perspective on the employer. It will help you decide if you really want to work there. Just because you interview with someone doesn't mean that you want to work with that person day in and day out. You need to make sure that this job will be a good fit for you, too. Yes, you need to interview the employer while you are there, too. Before you go, think about what your criteria for a great job are, and make a list of your own questions to ask. The employer knows that you will have questions, too. Some even ask, "Do you have any questions?" This is something else you can practice ahead of time.

Networking

You don't have to do this alone. In fact, you shouldn't try to do it all by yourself. You need someone to help you edit your résumé or CV and someone to help you role-play your interview questions. There are plenty of other people who graduated at the same time you did. They were your colleagues in school, and they can be your colleagues now. If you work together, you can help each other.

Build on your old connections and stay in touch with your fellow students. Add to your network by attending professional meetings in your field. You can even volunteer for your professional organization as a way to grow your career. Someone you meet at a seminar can give you a tip about a new job. You may meet a future employer there.

GLOSSARY

ACCREDITED Officially recognized as meeting the essential requirements.

AFFINITY In chemistry, the tendency for two substances to combine.

ALLOY A substance composed of two or more metals or a metal mixed with nonmetals.

ANTIBODIES Protein molecules produced by cells as a primary immune defense.

BIOINFORMATICS The branch of information science concerned with large databases of biochemical or pharmaceutical information.

DISSERTATION A thesis written by a candidate for the degree of doctor of philosophy (Ph.D.).

FERMENTATION A chemical reaction that causes an organic molecule to split into simpler substances.

FLASK A glass bottle with a rounded body and a narrow neck, used in laboratory experimentation.

HERBICIDE A substance or preparation for killing plants.

INHIBITOR In chemistry, a substance that decreases the rate of or completely stops a chemical reaction.

INTERNSHIP Any official or formal program to provide practical experience for beginners in an occupation or profession.

PATENT The exclusive right granted by a government to an inventor to manufacture, use, or sell an invention for a certain number of years.

PHARMACEUTICAL Of or relating to drugs or a pharmacy.

POLYMER A compound of high molecular weight with many small molecules.

POSTDOCTORAL The study or professional work undertaken after the receipt of a doctorate.

PROTEOMICS The branch of biochemistry concerned with the structure and analysis of the proteins occurring in living organisms.

REMEDIATION The correction of something bad or defective.

SYNTHESIS In chemistry, the forming or building of a more complex substance or compound from elements of simpler compounds.

TITRATION The measurement of the volume or concentration of a solution by adding liquid.

FOR MORE INFORMATION

American Association for the Advancement of
    Science (AAAS)
1200 New York Avenue NW
Washington, DC 20005
(202) 326-6400
Website: http://www.aaas.org
The American Association for the Advancement of
    Science is an international nonprofit organiza-
    tion dedicated to advancing science around the
    world.

American Registry of Professional Animal
    Scientists (ARPAS)
1800 S. Oak Street, Suite 100
Champaign, IL 61820-6974
(217) 356-5390
Website: http://www.arpas.org
The American Registry of Professional Animal Scien-
    tists provides certification of animal scientists
    through examination, continuing education, and
    commitment to a code of ethics.

Association for Women in Science (AWIS)
1321 Duke Street, Suite 210
Alexandria, VA 22314
(703) 894-4490
Website: http://www.awis.org
The Association for Women in Science is the premiere
    leadership organization advocating the interests
    of women in science and technology.

Board on International Scientific Organizations (BISO)
Policy and Global Affairs
The National Academies
500 Fifth Street
Washington, DC 20001
(202) 334-2807
Website: http://sites.nationalacademies.org/pga/biso
The Board on International Scientific Organizations
   oversees a network of more than twenty U.S.
   national committees corresponding to the various International Council for Science scientific
   member bodies in an effort to strengthen U.S.
   participation in international scientific, engineering,
   and medical organizations.

Environmental Protection Agency (EPA)
1200 Pennsylvania Avenue NW
Washington, DC 20460
(202) 272-0167
Website: http://www.epa.gov
The EPA is a U.S. governmental agency whose mission
   is to protect human health by enforcing environmental regulations.

Intel International Science and Engineering Fair
   (Intel ISEF)
1719 N Street NW
Washington, DC 20036
(202) 785-2255
Website: http://www.societyforscience.org/isef

The Intel International Science and Engineering Fair is the world's largest international precollege science competition.

National Research Council (NRC)
1200 Montreal Road
Building M-58
Ottawa, ON K1A 0R6
Canada
(613) 993-9101
Website: http://www.nrc-cnrc.gc.ca/eng
The National Research Council is the government of Canada's premier organization for research and development. Working with clients and partners, it provides innovation support, strategic research, and scientific and technical services.

Websites

Due to the changing nature of Internet links, Rosen Publishing has developed an online list of websites related to the subject of this book. This site is updated regularly. Please use this link to access the list:

http://www.rosenlinks.com/STEM/Sci

FOR FURTHER READING

Belcher, Wendy Laura. *Writing Your Journal Article in Twelve Weeks: A Guide to Academic Publishing Success*. Thousand Oaks, CA: SAGE Publications, 2009.

Bloomfield, Victor A., and Esam E. El-Fakahany. *The Chicago Guide to Your Career in Science: A Toolkit for Students and Postdocs*. Chicago, IL: University Of Chicago Press, 2008.

Bolles, Richard N. *What Color Is Your Parachute? 2013: A Practical Manual for Job-Hunters and Career-Changers*. Berkeley, CA: Ten Speed Press, 2013.

Christen, Carol, and Richard N. Bolles. *What Color Is Your Parachute? For Teens, 2nd Edition: Discovering Yourself, Defining Your Future*. Berkeley, CA: Ten Speed Press, 2010.

The College Board. *Book of Majors 2013: All-New Seventh Edition*. New York, NY: College Board, 2012.

The College Board. *Campus Visits and College Interviews*. New York, NY: College Board, 2012.

The College Board. *College Handbook 2013: All-New 50th Edition*. New York, NY: College Board, 2012.

The College Board. *Get It Together for College, 2nd Edition: A Planner to Help You Get Organized and Get In*. New York, NY: College Board, 2011.

Curley, Robert, ed. *New Thinking About Pollution*. New York, NY: Rosen Publishing, 2010.

Dartnell, Lewis. *Astrobiology: Exploring Life in the Universe*. New York, NY: Rosen Publishing, 2011.

Doeden, Matt. *Conflict Resolution Smarts: How to Communicate, Negotiate, Compromise, and More*. Minneapolis, MN: Twenty-First Century Books, 2012.

Feibelman, Peter J. *A PhD Is Not Enough!: A Guide to Survival in Science*. New York, NY: Basic Books, 2011.

Gelb, Alan. *Conquering the College Admissions Essay in 10 Steps, Second Edition: Crafting a Winning Personal Statement*. Berkeley, CA: Ten Speed Press, 2013.

Germano, William. *From Dissertation to Book*. Chicago, IL: University Of Chicago Press, 2013.

Guttman, Burton. *Genetics: The Code of Life*. New York, NY: Rosen Publishing, 2011.

Harmon, Daniel E. *Internship and Volunteer Opportunities for Science and Math Wizards*. New York, NY: Rosen Publishing, 2013.

Kahaner, Ellen. *Great Communication Skills*. New York, NY: Rosen Publishing, 2008.

Peterson's. *Teens' Guide to College and Career Planning*. Lawrenceville, NJ: Peterson's, 2011.

Rogers, Kara, ed. *New Thinking About Genetics*. New York, NY: Rosen Publishing, 2010.

Roza, Greg. *Great Networking Skills*. New York, NY: Rosen Publishing, 2008.

BIBLIOGRAPHY

Andraka, Jack. "Winning the Top Award at Intel ISEF 2012 Kicks off Amazing Year for Jack Andraka." *Society for Science* blog, April 30, 2013. Retrieved August 6, 2013 (http://societyforscience.typepad .com).

Benderly, Beryl Lieff. "How to Succeed in Industry by Really Trying." *Science*, May 03, 2013. Retrieved August 6, 2013 (http://www.sciencemag.org).

Bourdon, Rebecca. "Remediation Hydrologist Interview." ISEEK Green, July 27, 2011. Retrieved August 6, 2013 (http://www.iseek.org).

BP Biofuels. "Why Biofuels?" BP Outlook 2030, January 2013. Retrieved August 6, 2013 (http://www .bp.com).

Federation of State Medical Boards and National Board of Medical Examiners. "United States Medical Licensing Examination." Retrieved August 6, 2013 (http://www.usmle.org).

Gomila, Billy. "Louisiana Students Bring Home Honors from International Science and Engineering Fair." LSU Media Center, May 30, 2012. Retrieved August 6, 2013 (http://www.lsu.edu).

Hansen, Randall S. "Preparing a Curriculum Vitae: Proven Success Strategies." Quintessential Careers. Retrieved August 6, 2013 (http://www.quint careers.com/curriculum_vitae.html).

Liptak, Adam. "Supreme Court Rules Human Genes May Not Be Patented." *New York Times*, June 13, 2013. Retrieved August 6, 2013 (http://www .nytimes.com).

Miller, Barbara. "Students from Palmyra, Susquenita

Bring Home Top Awards from International Science Fair." PennLive, May 22, 2013. Retrieved August 6, 2013 (http://www.pennlive.com).

National Institute of General Medical Sciences. "Medical Scientist Training Program." June 12, 2013. Retrieved August 6, 2013 (http://www.nigms.nih.gov/Training/InstPredoc/PredocOverview-MSTP.htm).

Perkins, Sid. "Teens Take Home Science Gold." Science News for Kids, May 17, 2013. Retrieved August 6, 2013 (http://www.sciencenewsforkids.org).

Roach, John. "17-Year-Old Builds Protein Decoder Tool that Could Lead to New Cancer Drugs." NBC News, March 13, 2013. Retrieved August 6, 2013 (http://www.nbcnews.com).

Roach, John. "Whiz Kid Grows Algae Under Her Bed, Wins Intel Science Fair." NBC News, March 13, 2013. Retrieved August 6, 2013 (http://www.nbcnews.com).

Savage, David G. "Supreme Court Rules Against Patenting Human Genes." *Los Angeles Times*, June 13, 2013. Retrieved August 6, 2013 (http://www.latimes.com).

Society for Science and the Public. "Intel ISEF." May 17, 2013. Retrieved August 6, 2013 (http://www.societyforscience.org/isef/).

Stahl, Elizabeth. "Laboratory Intern in Biofuels." Biotech Careers. Retrieved August 6, 2013 (http://biotech-careers.org/photo-journals/laboratory-intern-biofuels).

The Trustees of the University of Pennsylvania. "Medical Scientist Training Program." Retrieved August

6, 2013 (http://www.med.upenn.edu/mstp/index
.shtml).

Tucker, Abigail. "Jack Andraka, the Teen Prodigy of Pancreatic Cancer." *Smithsonian*, December 2012.
Retrieved August 6, 2013 (http://www.smithsonian
mag.com).

The University of Texas Southwestern Medical Center.
"M.D./Ph.D.–Medical Scientist Training Program."
Retrieved August 6, 2013 (http://www.utsouth-
western.edu).

U.S. Bureau of Labor Statistics. *Occupational Outlook
Handbook*. March 29, 2012. Retrieved August 6,
2013 (http://www.bls.gov/ooh).

U.S. Environmental Protection Agency. "Acid Rain."
December 4, 2012. Retrieved August 6, 2013
(http://www.epa.gov/acidrain).

Zimmerman, Eilene. "Hiring in Hydrology Resists
the Slump." *New York Times*, March 7, 2009.
Retrieved August 6, 2013 (http://www.nytimes
.com/2009/03/08/jobs/08start.html).

INDEX

About the Author

Anastasia Suen is the author of more than 160 books for children and adults. She has been watching STEM careers in action since growing up on the Space Coast in the early days of NASA. Her first published book was about the *Apollo 11* moon landing, and she has been writing about STEM for children, teens, and adults ever since. Suen lives with her family in Plano, Texas.

Photo Credits

Cover, p. 1 lightpoet/Shutterstock.com; pp. 4–5, 18–19, 106–107 Bloomberg/Getty Images; p. 10 Brendan Hoffman/Getty Images; pp. 12–13, 42–43 kali9/E+/Getty Images; pp. 14–15 © Santa Rosa Press Democrat/ZUMA Press; pp. 20–21 Carsten Peter/Speleoresearch & Films/National Geographic Image Collection/Getty Images; p. 23 Andrew Douglas/Radius Images/Getty Images; pp. 26–27 Carsten Peter/National Geographic Image Collection/Getty Images; pp. 28–29 U.S. Navy photo by MC3 Devin Wray; p. 30 Robert Kneschke/Shutterstock.com; pp. 34–35 Phil Degginger/Science Source; p. 36 Olga Miltsova/Shutterstock.com; pp. 38–39, 44, 48–49, 67, 94–95 © AP Images; pp. 46–47 The Christian Science Monitor /Getty Images; p. 53 Ken M Johns/Photo Researchers/Getty Images; p. 55 Tatiana Grozetskaya/Shutterstock.com; pp. 56–57 arek malang/Shutterstock.com; p. 60–61 racorn/Shutterstock.com; p. 62 John Smierciak/MCT/Newscom; pp. 64–65 Monty Rakusen /Cultura/Getty Images; pp. 70–71 Jaime Razuri/AFP/Getty Images; pp. 76–77, 81 Cultura Science/Matt Lincoln/Oxford Scientific/Getty Images; pp. 78–79 Thomas Tolstrup/Iconica/Getty Images; p. 85 Pasieka/Oxford Scientific/Getty Images; pp. 90–91 Life in View/Science Source; pp. 98–99 Scott Barbour/Getty Images; pp. 108–109 Klaus Vedfelt/Riser/Getty Images; pp. 110–111 Steve Debenport /E+/Getty Images; cover and interior design elements © iStockphoto .com/kemie, iStock/Thinkstock, © iStockphoto.com/julioechandia, © iStockphoto.com/alwyncooper.

Designer: Brian Garvey; Editor: Nicholas Croce;
Photo Researcher: Cindy Reiman